winner
michigan writers cooperative press
**2024 poetry contest**

# BONES AND BREATH
Ruth Zwald

Copyright © 2024 by Ruth Zwald. All rights reserved.

Michigan Writers Cooperative Press
P. O. Box 2355
Traverse City, Michigan 49685

ISBN-13: 978-1-950744-19-0

Book cover design by Amy Hansen

# Contents

## BONES

| | |
|---|---|
| Canticle Of The Bones | 3 |
| Chopping Down Stones | 4 |
| My Father Converses With Heaven | 5 |
| Times Two | 7 |
| grief like this | 8 |
| The Bone Tree | 9 |
| My Mother's China | 10 |
| Listening To My Grandparent's Bones | 11 |
| Seventeen Inches | 13 |
| This Kind Of Autumn | 14 |
| On Hearing the Lamentation of Owls | 15 |
| Swallowing The Sun | 16 |

## AND BREATH

| | |
|---|---|
| Take The Feathers And The Bones | 19 |
| We Never Were That Kind of Family | 20 |
| Ley Lines | 21 |
| Looking For Your Light, I Set Out | 22 |
| The Way My Breath Goes | 23 |
| the long grasses of late summer | 24 |
| The Healing That Can Only Happen When The Light Bends This Way | 26 |
| If I Were A Contestant On The British Baking Show Holiday Edition And We Were Instructed To Make A Festive Bread From Our Ethnic Tradition | 27 |

| | |
|---|---|
| "Let us be the ancestors our descendants will thank" | 28 |
| Hang Lanterns From The Trees | 30 |
| tender mercies | 31 |
| We Live Like This | 32 |

## EPILOGUE

| | |
|---|---|
| When It Is My Turn To Go | 35 |
| Acknowledgements | 39 |
| About the Poetry Judge | 40 |
| About the Author | 41 |
| About Michigan Writers Cooperative Press | 42 |
| Other Titles Available | 43 |

# BONES AND BREATH

*Sitting among the bones of those who are gone.
Resting in the time between the sorrows.
Creating a future tethered to the past.
I breathe.*

# BONES

# Canticle Of The Bones

Blessed be bones as night befalls
shadows crowding the soul—
it is time for bones to speak.

Sing out, o bones, the stories of ancestors:
sinew to my sinew, tugging at the past,
visible in this skeleton of a life.

Rattling bones, waking me fearful in the dark
to loss expecting to be released
and remains awaiting a scattering.

Tell out, o marrow of bones, where
unseen maladies devour
white blood cells of imagination.

Lead on, all ye dancing bones who stare
at the veil, swaying to the seductive sound
of days end and journey beyond.

Cast the bones and let them scatter
in patterns sacred, pointing to the now
and the deep dark ache.

Make me a keeper of bones.

# Chopping Down Stones

The axe is sharp.
No chainsaw for this task.
Just swing,
breathe,
swing,
breathe.

These stones are old. Wouldn't you think
that makes them more fragile?

My father used to take the handsaw to the woods
in winter and down firewood to sell.
Back,
forth,
breathe.

My father is fragile.

I will gather these chopped stones
in to a pyre
of hard memories
and strike
a match of belonging.

# My Father Converses With Heaven

It was in those last months
after you celebrated your 100th birthday that you began
the questions about heaven—

*How will I find my way?*

You asked it of your wife as the two of you dwell
in the simplicity of morning coffee
and she told you to look for your guardian angel
because Lord knows you have one

like that time the silo auger swung and knocked you out
and there was that day a fire threatened the barn
and then there was that spring when the creek flooded
and you had to rescue cows.

You listened, squinting to see but your stubborn skepticism
left a furrow on your soul through those long months
as time softened with no cows no crops to worry over

only the slowing
of your breathing
and your blue eyes whispering to me

*Am I dying?*

Yes.
Oh how you love this earth and every season
passing. Often enough in the past years you tell me

*I would do it all over again - life is so interesting.*

It was in those last days
as those who love you most come
and tell stories of what they remember
and they leave

[…]

back to their own stories
while you drift in a place where the sun
no longer warms your bones.

*How do I?*

It was in those last moments when the twilight
is silent, that I pick up the memoir you had written
reaching for the deeper comfort of your own words.

I read aloud coming to this story - before
electricity, before your sister died from influenza,
before your family lost the farm during the depression.
It is winter. You are eight.

You get home from school as dusk settles
heading to the drafty barn where your father
(you were always so close to your dad)

was milking the handful of cows.
Finishing your chore of hand pumping the water
from the cistern to the cattle trough

you lie in the warm hay
in the dark of the barn and fall asleep to the melody
of the milking, of your father.

When your dad wakes you he takes down
the lantern hanging from the barn hook casting long shadows
over the two of you as you walk back to the house.

You remember every detail. Oh papa
I sigh through my whispering blue eyes
that's how you find your way.

Just lie down in the hay and sleep—
your dad will come and gently wake you—
take down the lantern—

together you will walk through the dark—
till you reach the house—
where everyone is waiting.

# Times Two

**1.**

In the deep quiet of predawn, my father left his body / worn
out / left his sun stained skin / his regrets / his stories behind.

It happened like this. The phone startles me awake / by the time
I reach my father's room at the nursing home, there is a candle lit
by his door / his small body is being covered. They could have
called me sooner / the nursing home prefers to protect family members
from the untidiness of death. It is a strange lonely sorrow in the night,
his last breath echoing unattended / solitary.

My mothers room is down the hall / I go to wake her. In the dark quiet
we make our way. She in a wheelchair and I on my feet, we enter
to say goodbye. Goodbye to the body / to the memories stacked on
memories layered like the bales of hay in the barn. Goodbye to
the debris of disappointment / of ancient anger. Goodbye to hard work in
sunshine / to the cold, cold winters. All of it finished in this deep / quiet way.

**X2.**

The day after my father's ashes are tucked in the earth he loved, I tuck
my worn out mother in her bed / promising that I will be back soon.
My exhausted mother naps, her c-pap machine creating white noise /
easier breath. I am heading to my own home / my own layers of life /
hours away where my breath can be a bit deeper without grief in the very air.

It happened like this. When I am almost home, the phone startles the driving trance.
My niece tearfully tells that she went to be with my mother / she was gone / left her body.
My niece found her with the c-pap removed from her face / freeing her mouth
as if seeing something / as if needing to speak. So just like that, my mother
knew all her goodbyes had already been spoken / she let go / swift /
her last breath echoing unattended / solitary.

It is winter now, deep and quiet. Stories wait to be told.

# grief like this

things that the wind
blows down
I live in

the large pinecones scattered
I gather / nestle in
to sleep for awhile

broken branches large and small
shelter me as I cook
my breakfast / plan my day

how I will crochet the released leaves
hooking their beauty / stitching a lap blanket
for the long nights ahead

I can do this
I have time

I can do this
no one is watching
or maybe everyone is watching

# The Bone Tree

My father wished to be like the maple tree—not to be the tree itself
but the deep roots living long, keeping his spine supple as branches
bend in winds, keeping his trunk sturdy so as not to break with

unexpected gusts. There is a sorrow in this poem, in the bones of it.
"Feel this," my friend says on the school bus one late fall morning,

this bump near her collarbone like a hard knot on a tree, foreign
to her softness and she thought it an injury from water skiing last summer but
it wasn't, and before the trees turned that next autumn, she was gone.

Then just before our anticipated high school senior year, my red-haired friend
vanished as another vehicle crashed head on into hers. I went to see

the twisted remains of her car but couldn't bring myself to view hers until
they were buried deep beneath the oak tree at the Catholic Church cemetery.
Oh and how my list of loss could go on but you see now where this is going.

There is a sorrow in this poem, a whispered weeping in the woods for stripped
bark, for sweet sap stopped mid flow, for old trees now gone forever.

Here is an unanswerable question: why lightning strikes one tree and not
the other. My wounded answer: gather the sacred wood from the lightning tree,
burn its flame against the dark, losses lining up to be remembered in the embers

with a song of honor and a drumbeat of hope that this beating heart
can heal, these bones knit kind, made strong, bend to meet another day.

# My Mother's China

And then there is her china. I spread it out on the table
as I wonder what to do with these things my mother touched.
Actually she has three sets of dishes—
the good china, the extra china, and the everyday plates and bowls.
But it is the good china that feeds my soul.
A simple pattern of apple blossoms pink on gray
on each plate that she taught me to place so that the stem
on the blossom pointed down when I set the table for company.
*It should look like the blossom branch spreads out in front of the eye of the guest.*
Large plates, salad plates, dessert plates, gravy boat, serving bowls, coffee cups.

My mother took such pride in table and food and creating
hospitality as the world tumbled toward screens and convenience.
Tablecloths and festive napkins every holiday and birthday. Come sit. Goblets
filled with ice and sweet tea. Give thanks. Platters of roasted meat. Potatoes
heaped. Vegetables with browned butter. A salad of seven layers. Jello
in cut glass bowls. Pass the food. Fresh baked bread. Extra butter
and homemade jam. Have some more. My mother is extravagant
in this way of loving us.

What to do with all these things that hold my mother to me?
I am not a keeper, moving as I do on the slightest breeze
of remembering that nothing lasts forever.
I wish I was an artist. Could find the courage and vision to break
the breakables. Could take the shards of that life and create a mosaic,
maybe gluing them down on a table top or a piece of garden art. Fit the pieces
together in a new way. Let the stems of the blossoms point a different
direction. But I am not that kind of artist. If I tried, it would only be a mess.

I am a mess. My grief spread out and who even uses cups and saucers
these days. Plus, I have my own set of china. I have my own.

# Listening To My Grandparent's Bones

## ELISA

She couldn't be sure what it was that caused the coldness to spread / swallowing her fingers. Her fingers are usually so nimble / tatting lace / embroidering flowers on plain muslin pillowcases / hemming a dress / darning socks.

But now her hands lay idle in her lap / her needles stuck straight in the pin cushion.

Maybe it is the light causing it / the light is different in Iowa. Kerosene lamps cast shadows on the long nights / everything looks foreign. She is from the city / electricity in your home / to stitch / read by / electricity on the streets / letting the night become familiar.

But here on the farm we make do / make do without.

Maybe it is the mud causing it / all the mud in the Iowa months between winter and summer / mud caking barn boots / mud stepped through to get to the wagon / mud that makes gathering eggs a slippery mess / even the eggs in the nest boxes are covered in mud.

You can't go anywhere / without mud as companion.

Maybe it is her new husband's fault / taking her away from her home. Her sisters told her that she better take this suitor or at 31 she would end up a spinster / caring for their widowed mother / keeping her long hours as a seamstress at the fur company.

But her husband has kind hands / so it can't be his fault.

Or maybe it is simply being away from her sisters. Sisters who run their households together / sharing tasks / advising her on how to roll the pie crust / how to hang the laundry / plant the seeds / to can the pickles / how to hold back the dank cold.

They write letters / but she can't touch the hands that formed the words.

Or maybe it is her past trailing behind her to this new place / she tries so hard to be a farmer's wife / to be a helpmate / to forget her past / make a fresh start as her sisters would say / to trust that maybe God is good.

Whatever the cause / it doesn't seem to matter any more. The coldness is creeping up her arms / through her torso / tightening her heart / soon she will be unable to breathe.

[…]

## CHARLIE

I can put my large hands around her tiny waist / there is such fragility there seeping through her bones. I don't know how to hold her together anymore.

She is my ray of light / my touch of beauty / my place of rest at the end of the day of labor.

Maybe if I loved the farm more / she would learn to love it more. But my older brother is the real farmer. Feeding / milking / sowing / sheltering / harvesting / listening to clouds.

Farming is the only work my hands know. Yet sometimes when I hear the distant whistle of the steam engine / I dream of movement / of seeing different landscapes.

My sister reminds me that I am married now / need to settle down. Accept the way things are. She says things will get better when children come along / shouldn't that be happening soon?

But all I can see these days is my wife's slight bones. So why not move back to her family? There may be a place for me in the city / changing my overalls to trousers / my boots to shoes.

My hands are large / strong. You'd think I would know how to use them.

# Seventeen Inches

This grief of things left unsaid rumbles in the storm of memories
wondering why my tongue can't form words, why I swallow my longing.

These shadows of words create chasms of sorrow where I am not
brave enough not strong enough not enough to bring into the light

the fears unspoken, the currents of compassion and love harbored.
Now you are no longer here. If only feelings were action and words were balm.

The Shaman says the distance between our head and our heart is seventeen inches.
It is the one journey that takes a lifetime.

# This Kind Of Autumn

The leaves cling / hang on
this particular autumn
Other years they fall in a hurry
beauty littering the lawn
    But this year is green / we speak of it
    as we sit outside on a warm late afternoon
    in this late year of our lives

Whether the leaves stay or go
the nights are longer / the ghosts begin to roam

I can't say how many years ago this started
autumn / me / the ghosts

sometimes on the wind they rush through me
    sometimes in the night the door creaks
        sometimes they peak through the slats
            of the old barn during the twilight chores
                sometimes in the attic with the squirrels
                eavesdropping on the conversations

I wouldn't mind at least I think I wouldn't
if they appeared full form / spoke their mind
gave me a little advice
    how best to overwinter the root vegetables
    or how to hold my children's heaviness
        or how time is spinning
            or just a story about life where they are
                what God says about the green fall

But they are unattached to words / I can't seem
to get enough of them

# On Hearing the Lamentation of Owls

Through twilight I wander shadows past,
foraging memories through the fallen wet leaves

clinging to my shuffling shoes on an indiscernible path.
Trusting my other senses, my mouth tastes damp decay,

my ears sing stillness, my heart sprouts eyes
in the wisdom awake that this is the only way

to discern the dark. It is the season of bones,
of stripping to the skeleton of quiet grief -

this bleakness that makes it impossible
to take a deep breath without a deep ache forming

right at the place where my chest expands.
The days are so short, my sorrow so long

and where I have been matters not, it is where I am
and how, oh how, does one let go

into the deeper song, the keener eyesight, the swift silence.

# Swallowing The Sun

When I rise in the still dark
my eyes crusted with dreams
full of fret for my children my grandchildren
and a sorrow deeper than any one worry

When I rise in the still dark
because sleep is not a shelter
and there is no other way
but to get up
on my aching knees

When I rise in the still dark
my refuge is stepping outside
where birds sing to the day
no matter

When I rise in the still dark
outside I face east and wait

I face east and wait
greeting every tree every song every growing

I face east and wait
with a long lineage of seekers
for that moment
when the light
crawls over the horizon

I face east and swallow the sun

AND **BREATH**

## Take The Feathers And The Bones

Through the summer, I gather feathers scattered
in our yard. A soft bouquet of grays, browns,
blues, stripes, full of flight and breath.

In the fall, I sit with the feathers, quietly murmuring
memories that break my heart all over again.
The feathers, tender and kind, hum along.

In the winter, I gather bones from wherever
they show themselves, unearthing with the frosty
ground in the graveyard of my griefs.

In the spring, I carve the bones into talismans who choose
feathers to adorn their heads, then stand vigil to this one life
guided by all above, all beneath, all that has come before.

# We Never Were That Kind of Family

you know, the kind that reaches from the heavens
to communicate / the kind that turns from the stars

in their eyes / the kind of family that when your poem
is published / when you join a peace march / when you take

a risk to lead / the kind of family that asks about your
life / shows up / whispers in your ear / *now that is something*

I was wrong to think you would come alongside in that way

yet when the gladiolas are tall / five blooms on the stem
speak of a pink that is so soft it is comforting / yet when

the basket full of fresh picked green beans on my lap
snapping each one basking in the waning sun / yet when

I smell the dark rye bread baking / then later
slice / generously buttering its warmth

there you are / such unpredictable companions

# Ley Lines

Did you hear that interview on NPR—the author of a top-book-list-best-seller
sharing that she wrote every thought, crafted every line at a local coffee shop?
A necessity, she said, to step away from her life and in to another existence.

So here I am in the coffee shop, nibbling a scone, waiting for some time
for another existence to show up. But all that is happening is that I imagine how cozy
I would be in front of the wood stove with my hands wrapped around my favorite mug,

canonizing how rain turns in to snow on a quiet morning as the cat
trots by my side to the chicken coop where the hens articulate dawn
till I open their little door releasing them out in to the big world for the day.

And over there is the steady wood pile created from hours of hauling, splitting, stacking
and how I love every minute of that physical work. And over there the last
of the cabbages in the garden wait patiently for their existence to be complete.

I am devoted to the distractions. Setting the teapot to boil. Answering the need
of the fire for another log. Snatching a handful of black walnuts cracked last fall.
Scrolling through recipes till I find the best way to use the bountiful butternut squash.

# Looking For Your Light, I Set Out

Tell me of a season when your body
spoke only of malady and trial
and I will tell you of the winter
of my bones yearning for warmth

Tell me of an era when your sorrow was so deep
that your eyes could barely open to look upon it
and I will reveal to you the barren landscape
where I sojourned for months

Tell me of a turn when you wished to confess
the ways your shortcomings wounded others
and I will recite to you the story of the river that ofttimes
rushes through my body in this never ending cleansing

Tell me of the epoch of your betrayed relationships
with broken shards unmendable
and I will instruct you of the steadfastness of trees
as they bend in the winds while some branches snap

Tell me of a moment when all was balanced
your heart open and grateful
and I will sing to you the song of a sunrise
where the light softens all my edges

# The Way My Breath Goes

If God was God and I was Star
it would all be alright
because Star is part of something
expanding and visible in the universe.

If God was God and I was Ant
I question if it would be alright
for a whole existence to be the tedious
trek from food to home carrying burdens
much too large.

If God was God and I was Tree
well then maybe it would be alright
being a tall old sturdy kind of tree
the sequoia kind of tree that lives
among its own longer than even a tree
can imagine.

If God was God and I was Lightning
that would be more than alright
equal voiced to the divine stirring
wonder and awe in the heavens.

If God was God and I was Suffering
at least I would not be alone
holding hands with grief, abuse, disease,
depression, despair, loss upon loss
and oh the circle of hands keeps going
as we wonder if God is God.

If God was God and I was Me
it might not be alright all the time but still
there is the way color dances at sunset
the smell of cumin sautéing with onions
the touch on my skin of snow or rain or a hand
the way my breath goes in and out.

# the long grasses of late summer

in the early morning
the late summer slant of the sun

my breath and my feet keep pace with one another
jogging the trail around the prairie grass and marshland

native grasses bend sweetly across my path
everything beginning to let go slowly

feet wet with dew matching my forehead
amazingly not furrowed as I run

all summer this has been mine—this breath,
this path, this ease, this beauty
 .....
    pondering my ancestors as I often do
    wondering if any of them ever ran

    for the pleasure of muscle and movement
    for the necessity of moving toward healing

    wondering if they ever ran toward something
    or if the day was the day

    and the tasks were the tasks
    and the grief was the grief

    so you just kept moving
    this is what I wonder
 .....
the grasses are damp this morning and leaning as they do
soon my arms and legs are damp

the mornings are heavier this time of year
the warmth of the day starts to waken

but the feel, the sound, the sigh of these days
is changing as the slowness pulls me in

    ·····
        my lineage is stacked with hard workers
        dawn to dusk kind of workers

        men hand to the plow women back bent in the garden
        canner boiling on the wood cook stove

        preserving what could be preserved
        which they know is very little for not very long

  ·····
those long grasses leave their mark
grass seeds so cleverly

cling to my skin as they reach for a new place
hoping I will carry these freckles

to where they can flourish and spread
and be known by birds and blessings

  ·····
        pondering my ancestors as I often do
        these marks they left on my skin in my bones

        hoping I would carry them forward
        clever girl that I am

        plant their kindness their care for beauty
        to never stop working with whatever the day holds

# The Healing That Can Only Happen When The Light Bends This Way

the last of the green beans drop from browning vines
the sunflower bows toward earth with weight of seed and stalk
the tomato ripe and red warms the hand with snatched sunlight

the quilt grandma stitched tucks in with soft flannel sheets
the windows of the bedroom no longer hold the cricket chorus
the light lets go of day as leaves let go of tree

the taste of change is sharp on the tongue awakening hunger for quiet
the quiet stirs spectral shadows of things long past
the dreamtime is deeper than the breath at days end

the words wander scattering seeds gleaned in
the heavier soil of sound and soul

# If I Were A Contestant On The British Baking Show Holiday Edition And We Were Instructed To Make A Festive Bread From Our Ethnic Tradition

my 65-year-old hands would be kneading a Stollen dough
the recipe that my great-grandfather carried from Germany
in 1885 where he was a baker before immigrating
with this recipe enriched with butter and eggs and scalded milk and sugar
laden with stewed raisins and candied cherries


and I have no idea if my great-grandfather had success as a baker in Minnesota
and I have no idea how one would create such bread
without a heavy duty dough hook on the electric mixer
instead he had only a wood stove rising and baking loaves
in the cold, cold northern December darkness.


Now I am imagining my grandmother at 65 making this bread though then
not yet a grandmother as her only surviving child, my father, would not marry
till later in life, no grandchild for another seven Christmases of making Stollen
as her small body and slender hands pull and stretch the heavy dough
with a strength she was rarely given credit for.


On the baking show, the judge will look at my finished loaf
drizzled in powdered sugar—picking it up to feel the heft of it—
cutting it—admiring the fruit spread evenly throughout—
proclaiming it delicious—but judging
that the whole loaf is a bit plain.

# "Let us be the ancestors our descendants will thank"

*—Winona LaDuke, Environmentalist Farmer*

A few days before Christmas, I gather my six-year-old granddaughter to head to the snow covered hill for her first ever sledding.

> *Within a week, huge piles of snow melt, drifting into water.*
> *It will be raining as the new year begins.*

As we put on her snow pants, my granddaughter is anxious - excited by the new plastic sled with its tie-dye colors - but worried that maybe sledding isn't for her.

> *I am anxious. The world is warming. The meteorologist*
> *uses words like "unprecedented" and "drought" and*
> *"flooding" and I take a deep breath.*

I reassure her as we slip on her mittens and button down her hood. Today we are the only ones here. I sit her in the front of the sled, climbing in behind. She says, "Are you sure about this, grandma?" I tell her she can hang on to my legs.

> *I am sure about so little. I read books on climate change. I write letters*
> *of action to my legislators. I have swapped out lightbulbs. I recycle.*
> *I grow my own food to limit shipping.*

Down the hill we go, the deeper snow keeping us from going too fast. I let out a whoop as winter's chill hits our faces. There is no one here to celebrate this first. To admire how bravely we are sliding down the hill.

We get to the bottom of the hill. My granddaughter stands up quickly. Did it overwhelm her? Will she demand to go home? But she stands and declares loudly to the snow and the sled, "Well, that was enjoyable!"

We go down the hill several more times, ending up going backwards or spinning round and round as we make our way down. We laugh and squeal. At the bottom we say, "That was awesome!"

> *I am uncertain as to what this mild winter means. Will we be able to tap the trees with gratitude, boiling the sap into syrup? Will the pear trees and the newly planted peach trees be able to rest before they bloom?*

We sled until her toes get cold. Taking off her boots, I slip my mittens on her feet to warm them. She says I am silly, to put mittens on feet. Tucking the tie-dye sled in the back of my car, we head towards home and hot chocolate.

# Hang Lanterns From The Trees

In these shortest of days
I track my own footsteps in the snow
identifying the patterns of my boots
the sway of my gait
the direction I am heading
the purpose behind it all

In these longest of nights
when the fire burns against the dark
murmuring messages beyond warmth
constantly changing, consuming

piecing together the past
stitching my ancestor's stories
pulled taut to my own threads
in patterns created to hold the dark
in these shortest of days

In these shortest of days
I let the bread rise slowly
I let the snow fall ungrudgingly
use the last of the carrots from the garden
in a celebratory stew consumed
in the quiet of all things
in these longest of nights

## tender mercies

after decades of sorting years into heavy stacks of regrets / sorrows / struggle
I will stack up moments instead / surrounded by mercy
I bow in the rituals that compose my days

this ritual of receiving the sun when it breaks through the clouds

    of snow clinging to barren branches

    of a path before and behind me through the trees

this ritual of petting the cats

    of lighting the candle

    of holding the stones

    of stirring the soup

this ritual of fingers reaching in soil where carrots sleep

    of eyes lifted to the sunflowers full stance

this ritual of seasons passing in sound

    of lonely owl in winters moonlit night

    of chickadee calling in spring blossoms

    of mockingbird singing as lambs chase one another

    of sandhill crane's throaty cry as leaves turn

this ritual of the way her hand brushes my head whenever she walks past

    of watching the fire as I fall asleep

# We Live Like This

It happens every March—an early spring day sneaks in
and we stretch our hunched bones to reach for the sun.

And those of us who made it through the winter rub
our eyes of long sleeps and drowsy days,

washing winter from our hands in the sap the maple
trees gift us, we lick the sweetness clean to our hearts.

Cutting the dead growth from last year's golden marigold
stems, we marvel that the lemon balm is already green

and growing and spreading its exuberant self to mingle
with the tender tips of emerging lilies. And we can see

what the gardens will become if there is enough rain and if
we can keep bending over and if the last frost is kind enough.

And just like that, in one day of warmth, we leave behind all hushed
stories told in the dark nights and begin singing new ones.

# EPILOGUE

# When It Is My Turn To Go

I will make myself small
following my breath
deep until I almost disappear.

I will scoot out the door as someone comes in.
I will shimmy up the lilac bush where a hummingbird
abandoned a nest

and I will wear the nest as a hat
because most likely the wind will pick up
while I am on the journey.

I will have already dug out a kayak
from an enormous pinecone
and stowed it among the mushrooms in the woods.

My paddle is made from the wing
of the beautiful flicker that the cat caught and ate
last summer.

I will drag my kayak to a place where the sky is open
and then I will get in and be ready
for that moment.

The moment I am waiting for? Well, you know
when you stand at the water's edge and the sun
makes a trail across the water

and it is a trail that only you see
because of where you stand and the slant of the sun
and how the water meets you both—

that is the trail I am looking for but - not on the water.
The trail will appear among the night sky
and the stars will meet me there.

[…]

As I wait, I will try not to worry about the six realms
from the Tibetan Book of the Dead or about purgatory
or pearly gates, golden roads or judgement.

I will focus instead on tasting each delicious piece of my simple life
one last time—the sweetness of my family—the comfort of my love—
and the richness of the earth, the earth, the earth.

# Acknowledgements

With deep gratitude to the many readers of my writings through the years. Your wisdom and encouragement sustains me, and my words are richer because of you. You know who you are.

And gratitude to the editors of the journals in which the following poems appeared:

"Chopping Down Stones" first appeared in *Claw and Blossom*.
"Swallowing The Sun" first appeared in *Voices de la Luna*.
"Canticle of the Bones" first appeared in *Blood And Thunder*.
"My Father Converses With Heaven" first appeared in *Lifelines*.
"My Mother's China" first appeared in *Earth's Daughters*.
"Hang Lanterns From The Trees" first appeared in *Farmer-ish*.

# About the Poetry Judge

**Anita Skeen** is the author of six volumes of poetry: *Each Hand A Map* (1986); *Portraits* (1990); *Outside the Fold, Outside the Frame* (1999); *The Resurrection of the Animals* (2002); *Never the Whole Story* (2011); *When We Say Shelter* (2007), with Oklahoma poet Jane Taylor; and *The Unauthorized Audubon* (2014), a collection of poems about imaginary birds accompanied by the linocuts of anthropologist/visual artist Laura B. DeLind. With Taylor, she co-edited the literary anthology *Once Upon A Place: Writings from Ghost Ranch* (2008). Her poetry, short fiction, and essays have appeared in numerous literary magazines and anthologies. She is Professor Emerita in the Residential College in the Arts and Humanities at Michigan State University.

# About the Author

Words have always been a focus in **Ruth Zwald**'s life. From high school forensics to a spoken word choral group in college, to her professional life as pastor and social worker—words have been honored. When an astrologer told Ruth several years ago she had no "earth" in her birth sign, she set about to find ways to ground. Ruth plants gardens and helps raise sheep and chickens on her farm in West Michigan. She became a student of indigenous spirituality and now never misses a solstice or equinox turning. Ruth also began digging up words like she digs potatoes—unearthing thoughts and reconnecting to the creative and healing use of language. You can find out more about Ruth on her website: www.spiritlinkservices.com.

# About Michigan Writers Cooperative Press

This book was published in the spring of 2023 in a signed edition of 100 copies.

This chapbook is part of the Cooperative Series of the Michigan Writers Small Press Project, which was launched in 2005 to give members of Michigan Writers, Inc. a new avenue to publication. All of the chapbooks in this series are an author's first book in that genre. The Coop Press shoulders the publishing costs for the first edition, and writers share the marketing and promotional responsibilities in return for the prestige of being published by a press that prints only carefully selected manuscripts. Chapbook length manuscripts of poetry, short stories, and essays are solicited each year from members and adjudicated by a panel of experienced writers and a judge who is a specialist in a particular genre. For more information, please visit www.michwriters.org.

MICHIGAN WRITERS is an open-membership organization dedicated to providing opportunities for networking, professional growth, and publication for writers of all ages and skill levels in Northwest Michigan and beyond.

MANAGING EDITOR: Gail Wallace Bozzano

COVER DESIGN: Amy Hansen

# Other Titles Available
from Michigan Writers Cooperative Press

*The Grace of the Eye* by Michael Callaghan
*Trouble With Faces* by Trinna Frever
*Box of Echoes* by Todd Mercer
*Beyond the Reach of Imagination* by Duncan Spratt Moran
*The Grass Impossibly* by Holly Wren Spaulding
*The Chocolatier Speaks of his Wife* by Catherine Turnbull
*Dangerous Exuberance* by Leigh Fairey
*Point of Sand* by Jaimien Delp
*Hard Winter, First Thaw* by Jenny Robertson
*Friday Nights the Whole Town Goes to the Basketball Game*
    by Teresa J. Scollon
*Seasons for Growing* by Sarah Baughman
*Forking the Swift* by Jennifer Sperry Steinorth
*The Rest of Us* by John Mauk
*Kisses for Laura* by Joan Schmeichel
*Eat the Apple* by Denise Baker
*First Risings* by Michael Hughes
*Fathers and Sons* by Bruce L. Makie
*Exit Wounds* by Jim Crockett
*The Solid Living World* by Ellen Stone
*Bitter Dagaa* by Robb Astor
*Crime Story* by Kris Kuntz
*Michaela* by Gabriella Burman
*Supposing She Dreamed This* by Gail Wallace Bozzano
*Line and Hook* by Kevin Griffin
*And Sarah His Wife* by Christina Diane Campbell
*Proud Flesh* by Nancy Parshall
*Angel Rides a Bike* by Margaret Fedder
*Ink* by Kathleen Pfeiffer
*What Will You Teach Her?* by Megan Klco Kellner
*Bluetongue and Other Michigan Stories* by Ryan Shek
*The Mountain Ash* by Kathleen Rabbers
*This Blue Earth* by Sharon Bippus
*Upstairs, Listening* by Melinda LePere
*Twinkies* by Kathleen Quigley
*The Sound a Car Door Makes* by Natalie Tomlin

**Michigan WRITERS**

www.ingramcontent.com/pod-product-compliance
Lightning Source LLC
Chambersburg PA
CBHW020443090526
**44586CB00045B/831**